S0-DUW-857

OF YOUTH
AND
THE RIVER

The Mississippi Adventure of
Raymond Kurtz, Sr.

by
Raymond Kurtz, Sr.
as told to
Mark Scheel

Illustrations by
Pete Peterson

 ROYAL PRESS

First printing July, 1993
Second printing December, 1993

Copyright ©1993 by Raymond Kurtz, Sr.

All rights reserved. No portion of this book may be reproduced in
any form without written permission.

Library of Congress Cataloging-in-Publication Data

Kurtz, Raymond Sr.
Of Youth and the River
The Mississippi Adventure of Raymond Kurtz, Sr.

I. Scheel, Mark. II. Title.
93-85153

ISBN 0-9637680-0-x

Royal Press, P.O. Box 2032, Emporia, KS 66801

This book is dedicated to the memory of Julian Fink, the best friend a fella ever had, who taught me the value of "fun" apart from the love of adventure.

"... No sound save the rush of the river."

Ethel Lynn Beers—"The Picket Guard"

PREFACE

It was the eve of great change. The summer of 1938. The territorial exploits in Europe by Adolf Hitler edged the continent ever closer to World War II. America, under Roosevelt, still groped for a means of surmounting the Great Depression. And in the American heartland—on the plains, in the forests, along the mighty rivers—the last of the rustic frontier legacy neared an end. It was a time for savoring the wild's unspoiled freedom. A time, too, for cherishing last innocence.

On July 14 of that year, Raymond Kurtz, a Richmond, Minnesota youth of 19, began what was to become a historic adventure. In a sailboat of his own design, he set out to become the first person ever to travel solo, without an auxiliary engine, the navigable length of the Mississippi River. Two months and 2,100 miles later he succeeded, docking at the Canal Street wharf in New Orleans.

His experiences along the way, colorful and frequently life-threatening, call to mind the writings of one of his favorite authors, Mark Twain. Following the occasion of the fiftieth anniversary of his trip, Kurtz decided to retell his Mississippi adventure, event by event. This, in his own words, is his story.

M. S.

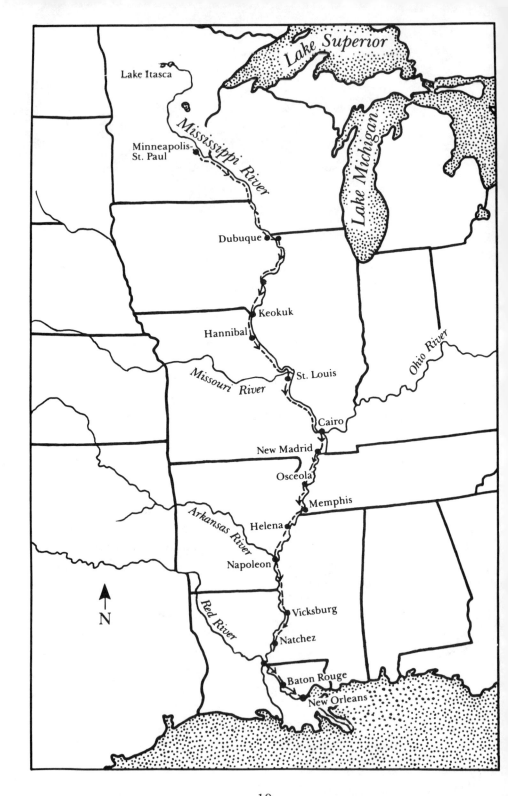

Putting the sailboat "The Minnesota" through its paces prior to commencing the trip down the Mississippi River, July 1938. (Raymond Kurtz in photo.)

Raymond Kurtz welcomes friends aboard his newly completed sailboat at the family resort near Richmond, Minnesota.

Nineteen-year-old Raymond Kurtz and his sailboat, "The Minnesota," upon arrival in New Orleans on September 14, 1938.

DOCKS IN N. O. AFTER SAILING DOWN RIVER

Jaℓ 14 - 1938

RAYMOND KURTZ

Sunburned, freckled and with calloused hands, a 19-year-old youth from Richmond, Minn., docked his 18-foot catrig sailboat at the head of Canal street this morning and announced his home of two months "for sale."

He is Raymond Kurtz and he'll proudly tell you he made the boat himself, "especially for the trip to New Orleans." Starting from St. Paul, Minn., alone in his cabin sailboat "with $5 worth of canned goods and $11.05 in my pocket," Kurtz averaged 24½ miles a day from St. Paul to Cairo and 40 miles per day from Cairo to New Orleans.

An admirer of Mark Twain's characters, especially Tom Sawyer, Kurtz, who says he will be a senior at Eden Valley High school if and when he gets back, can lay claim to quite a few adventures himself.

Among his experiences, Kurtz said, was an attack of malaria and a miraculous escape from death under a paddle wheel as he fell

Please turn to Page 2

Docks Here--

Continued from Title Page

off a barge into the Mississippi river. Then, too, if one can consider eating new foods like sweet potatoes and rice with gravy as experiences, then, the Minnesota lad lays claim to these, too.

It was canned goods and cooked corn meal for the adventurer, he complained, "and I grew darn tired of it. People along the river were very nice and donated lots of things to me," he said.

Why he took the trip? "Well, I thought it would be an education to see new places," he said, "and I'm going to spend a few days here until I sell my boat."

Seated on the steps of the post-office building today the Minnesota adventurer read letters from home, the first he received since he began the trip two months ago today. They were from relatives, his mother, and "a letter of congratulations from the Commercial Club."

With the boat for a home Kurtz will remain here "until someone offers a fair price for the boat." Then its back to Riverside resort, home and mother. Then, too, school started September 6 and the life of Tom Sawyer is for books and not for the 19-year-old youth of 1938.

14

Raymond Kurtz as he appears today, manager and operator of Royal Drain Cleaning in Emporia, Kansas.

OF YOUTH AND THE RIVER

The Mississippi Adventure of Raymond Kurtz, Sr.

OF YOUTH AND THE RIVER

I

Well now . . . I'd like to start off by saying that I'm much obliged for the help in taking all this down and writing it up. I've never been much of a one for trying to write things down—and I appreciate help along those lines—but I was always a talker. (laughter) That was my strong suit. I could always tell a good tale, and loved doin' it!

When I was just a youngster, we moved off the farm in North Dakota after my father died. He used to have a homestead out there. And we relocated in Minnesota. I was the eleventh of twelve children. And the machine age was just coming in, and the horse age was just going out. And that was an ideal time of the century to be born because there was so many things changing and taking place in a person's life and everywhere. You didn't realize it at the time, but you get the hindsight and look back on it, and you can see all the advantages there was.

I was a country boy. And I considered that a favorable advantage. I liked being in the country. I liked the woods, and animals, and things like that. The nearest boy my age to play with was about two miles in any direction from me. So I was a bit of an isolated country boy, but I had a lot to make up for it. I had a river, called the Sauk River, and I lived on a summer resort on the Horseshoe Chain of Lakes. There was twenty-two lakes in my back yard, plus all the woods that was surrounding it.

When we moved into the territory in the fall of 1926 off of the prairie farm, it was the difference of day and night. It was fantastic— the woods were so thick that there was places where the sun couldn't even shine through. You'd get in there and it was dusk at midday. Just that much coverage. And the wild fruit was so tremendous that it staggers your imagination. We would think nothing of going out and taking a boat and rowing down through the lakes. We'd land someplace back in the wilds shoreline, go back into the woods and pick chokecherries by the bushel basketful. Now that's a little berry smaller than the tip of your little finger, and we'd pick those by the *bushel* basketful. And not one basket but *several* of 'em! I had a younger sister and two older sisters and an older brother still at home, so there was five of us. And while us kids went out and picked, my mother would stay home and can.

And then there was the raspberries. We had a big island out in one of the lakes, and it was called Crane Heaven. Basically, it was called Crane Island, but the original name was Crane Heaven. And it was full of these tremendously big elm trees. They went towering up into the sky—just dozens of 'em—and in the tops of these elm trees the cranes had been nesting for who knows how long. Through the centuries. There'd be two or three nests in each tree, just depending on how they branched out. And you could walk underneath 'em and look up at those birds at night, you know, coming in there feeding their young. The foliage underneath the trees would be all white from the droppings, almost like snow. And I tell you, it was just like being in some sort of strange land.

But what I mentioned about these cranes for was the berries. They had carried in raspberry and blackberry seeds on their migration. They'd transplanted them as they flew across and dropped their droppings, and they had a growth of raspberries. Oh, you wouldn't believe it—all around the rookery area and spread on across the island. We could go in there and pick these wild raspberries by the gallon, and they were so good they'd just defy description. And in the spring there was this wild strawberry. They were down in the grass and we'd find them in clusters and pick them. And they had so much flavor in them—why, a whole dish of your tame strawberries wouldn't have much more flavor than just one of those little wild berries. When you bit into it, why, your saliva glands would literally explode!

And something else I almost forgot—gooseberries. There was gooseberry bushes all over. In the pastures, out in the open, as well as in the woods. There were places that they were so thick, you walked in paths, had to maneuver around through them, picking the berries. I could eat 'em with the spiney things on, just throw 'em in my mouth and eat away. You built up a kind of resistance to a lot of that stuff, because you'd eaten these things all the time, see.

Then, too, in the spring the woods were always chock-full of flowers. The grass didn't grow back in the woods because the cover was too heavy. They had a heavy leaf fall, and this mulch on the ground. And these flowers would push right up through these leaves. Dutchman's-breeches. Bloodroots. Honeysuckle. And touch-me-nots—right on down the line, you know. The woods was just full of 'em. Oh yeah, and hazelnuts. You could go out and pick wild hazelnuts. And I remember how I'd eat my dinner, and then I'd go out in the woods and have my desserts fresh off the bushes and trees!

And another thing I really enjoyed was all the small wild birds. These birds needed thick cover and they nested in small bushes like the gooseberry and raspberry and chokecherry bushes. And I remember I used to, about once a day or so, I made a tour through the woods and places where I'd seen these different nests of all these different kinds of birds. Robins, blackbirds, wild canaries, tree sparrows, whatever. I'd go from one nest to the other, stand and walk by 'em and look in and watch. I'd find the nests when they built 'em and then I'd follow it through until the birds were hatched and flown. Never bothered anything, but just enjoying the contact.

Now when I was younger and I wasn't too sharp on some of these things, the mother of the brood would see me coming, and she would drop out of the nest to the ground, and then she would flutter with her feathers all puffed out. She'd flutter, and I would pounce, and she'd just flutter out of my reach. I'd pounce again (laughter) . . . and, of course, the more I pounced, the farther she'd get me from the nest. Then all of a sudden she'd fly away real good. And I didn't catch on. I was real young when I first started learning these things.

But another thing, too, was these turtledoves. Watchin' the young birds grow up and fly. They're beautiful birds. And the robins would build right on our porch and the wrens right in the porch posts. That was just accepted as a matter of course, everyday comings and goings.

So—that was my life, as a youngster. You couldn't blame me for enjoying bein' a country boy. But I knew that it was all gonna come to an end sometime; I knew everything comes to an end. And I often wondered, how is this gonna end? How am I gonna *feel* when it comes to an end? And you know, it all came to an end real quick. Just like nobody's business. When the Japs bombed Pearl Harbor, that's when *everything* came to an end. Our whole world literally blew apart, and it came back together—we picked up the pieces and started puttin' it back together. And all of these things were gone when I came home after the war. The place was grown up with buildings and trailer courts and so forth. A lot of the bushes and trees these birds had nested in were torn out and landscaped. The wild shoreline, a lot of the wildest stuff, was now in lawns and summer homes. Even homes they lived in year round, summer cabins they'd had winterized and everything. Some of the wildest territory that you could go into was now just turned into *lawns!* And it had all changed in such a short period of time.

But anyway, getting on to the beginnings of the Mississippi trip. While I was on the summer resort in the early days, there was a doctor, a country medical doctor. And he would come out, along with a dentist named Reichert, to our resort. One of them might rent a cabin and then they would come out in the evenings. You know. Their wives would be out during the day, and the kids would be enjoying the lake shore and so forth. And the men would come out at night.

And they'd bring along their fine rifles and gear, repeaters and automatics, you know. Something that I would dream about, but know I'd never own. But they didn't come out to shoot things—they just came out to *shoot.* If there was a red squirrel or something like that in a tree, instead of shooting it, they'd shoot all around it. (laughter) Just for the sport of shooting, they'd clip limbs all around him. That old red squirrel would head for his hole in a tizzy. There were squirrels all over the place. Why, if I wanted a squirrel, I could shoot one from my porch. I mean they was just that plentiful. They'd lay up there on a big old elm limb and tease at you. You stuck your rifle out, and they'd put the limb between you and them and just keep right on teasin' you. If you moved around to the other side, they just moved right on around too. Of course, the trick of doing that, if you wanted to get one, was to take a chunk of wood and stand back where they was gonna come around. Then bounce that wood across the ground. And when the old squirrel moved around, you'd get him, see.

Anyway, this medical doctor made quite an impression on me.

He was truly a compassionate man. His name was Doctor Koop, and he was a handsome young fella, kind of stocky built and in good physical condition. Had a thin mustache, and a "citified" wife. And he always had a chauffeur for his coupe. Well, I'd have to say it was from him, more than anywhere else, that my idea about a boat trip first got its start.

He told me about how he and a friend, a buddy of his, canoed the upper Mississippi River during the summer when they was between school. And I'll never forget—one of the things he said . . . you haven't canoed until you can stand up in a canoe and battle it out between you and your buddy with a pair of canoe paddles. (laughter) He says, you haven't canoed until you've done that. And I thought that sounded kind of peculiar that a couple buddies would do that. Well, I canoed with one of the best buddies I've ever had in my life. And, hey, we didn't stand up in the canoe and battle—we had a little more sense. We went ashore. (laughter) I'll have to tell you about that sometime; we'll call that the Second Battle at the Fort Pillow Bluffs. But, anyway. I heard him talk a little bit about canoeing and things like that, and it got into my mind. I thought, hey, I'd like to do that; that sounds real interesting. I was real young then. I imagine around ten years of age.

When I first came to Minnesota, to the summer resort, I looked out the upstairs window. And I could see a gap in the trees and a big stretch of water. It was raining and there was a clearing between the rain and the sunshine. And I'll never forget that; that's still a picture in my mind to this day. When a little prairie boy came into land like that and saw the water for the first time.

Then this other boy that lived on the resort that we'd bought the property from, he took me down to the beach. And hey, you know, you couldn't hardly pull me away from there. I was just fascinated by the water.

Now another thing I remember from that same time—just as clear as the day it happened—had to do with an old-timer they called "Cooney." That being 1926, an old-timer was from a long time before that, of course. And this Cooney and his wife had a cabin down the river through the narrows. He came up to the resort one Sunday to get some minnows. So when he got his minnows and started back down toward the narrows, I stood there on the shore watching him row. And I tell you, my chin musta' been clear down to my tummy button. From

our landing out to the narrows it was about a half mile, and I looked at him rowing across that expanse of water in that tiny little boat. And I knew I must have seen the bravest man in all this entire world, takin' that little boat out into all that water! But you know, ironically, my buddy and I started from that exact same spot and canoed all the way down the Mississippi River in to the Gulf of Mexico several years later. That was my *second* trip down the Mississippi.

But the first time, I went alone. In my own sailboat. And it was this doctor who'd put it in my head. Now to begin with, I was gonna have one of my buddies go with me. Wardo. His dad was the blacksmith in town. So we left in the fall of 1937 to follow the harvest and earn some money. Well sir, he didn't have near the ambition I had. The old freight train pulled up at a crossing, slowed down at a crossing, slow enough so I could jump off, and I jumped off and landed on my face in the ditch, and my buddy went on home. So that ended that, uh, partnership. So then I had another buddy—this one was nicknamed Pop. And he worked for us on the resort and things like that. And he was supposed to go. But then he decided that he didn't want to go that year; if I'd wait till next year, he'd go then. But hey, I wasn't for waiting. I was for going. So—since I couldn't find anybody to go with me, I went *alone*. (laughter)

Now there was this old neighbor lady who had an old wood boat in her barn. It was just an old open boat about 18 feet long. And her nephew Jay said she'd sell it for five dollars. Well, I jumped at the offer, and I hauled the boat out on a set of buggy wheels to Horseshoe Lake. I let it soak for a few days to stop the leaks, and then I rowed it north, around under a bridge, and on down south to the landing at our resort. And I set it upside down on sawhorses and went to work.

I fashioned a mast out of a tall, straight pine I cut off my brother-in-law's farm. Put on a tin bottom and soldered the seams. And, of course, I had to make me a rudder. Then I built a deck and cabin. And I'm telling you, I even put glass in the cabin windows and built a door on the back that locked! (laughter) I was real proud of that. Painted the whole thing orange trimmed in black. And the sail I had custom made by a tent and awning company.

Now there was the butcher's son in the area who had a knack for lettering. So I had him paint her name on the bow—*The Minnesota*. That's what I called her. And I christened her with a bottle of cream.

So anyway, when it came time to set out, I loaded on my gear and what provisions I was taking—some canned goods, fishing tackle and a rifle. I had a compass, too, and corn meal, and an old portable victrola. Things like that, you know. And eleven dollars in cash. And I had the boat hauled by truck to Saint Paul, to the Jackson Street docks where the Capitol excursion boat lands. Slid it down the steps into the Mississippi River and put my mast on. There was a few people around there—an old sailor and a couple of kids. They helped get everything lined up. And sometime in the afternoon, around four or five o'clock, why, by golly, I was on my way down the Mississippi River!

II

So—I was underway. I was drifting down the river. And the
first thing that came by me was a steamboat. Well, I'd heard stories
about these BIGGGG waves that these steamboats throw up. That they
could swamp a small boat easy if you didn't watch out. And so I held
my breath tight and kept my eyes peeled as the steamboat went by. I
think, as I remember, ironically, it was the *Huck Finn* or the *Tom
Sawyer*. I'd have to check my records on that. But anyway, it went by,
and I pulled on in behind it, and I said, hey, this ain't too bad. The
waves weren't all *that* big.

But the farther I got from the steamboat, the *bigger* the waves
got. (laughter) That's the way it is with riverboats, paddle wheelers, I'd
find out; the farther you get behind 'em, the higher the waves get.
Because they're pushing current with the current, and that throws a
swell up, and it's a long rolling one. But if they're pushing against the
current, they're throwing a swell up too, but it's a shorter and steeper
one. And so I got myself a reasonable little shaking up. But I thought
after it was all over with, it was still fine. Nothing too much to worry
about. So I had that behind me—I'd weathered my first steamboat.

And so I drifted on down the river. It was a nice . . . quiet . . .
sunny afternoon. Wasn't a ripple hardly on the water, and I was drifting
with the current. Along toward sundown I came to a place where the
river divided. It was an island, and the channel went around to the
right. I pulled in behind the island, and I camped on a little stretch of

beach. And there was a farm up through the pasture there; you know, this farmland comes right down to the river for a long ways. And so, that was my first night on the river.

I thought, well, everything's just great now. I'm gonna just keep right on a-rollin'. Thought I had it made. Because I didn't get swamped by the first steamboat. (laughter) And I'd navigated a few miles of navigation water that I'd never done before. But, I had something to consider yet—how was I gonna get through the locks? And the next afternoon, boy oh boy, I came face to face with the first locks.

I had a twenty-five cent whistle that had two cylinders in it. In other words, it blew a double note. And, uh, so I looked at the locks. And I thought, boy, here's gonna be a real trial now; if I can't get through these things, it's gonna be rough getting my sailboat around it. So I got my two-bit whistle out and I blew on that thing a couple of times. There was no sight of anybody on the locks or anything. Just snags in the water here and there. Water had backed up. The channel had gotten bigger and the current had gotten lighter. And all of a sudden I see those big old lock doors opening. So I hustled myself in. And somebody threw me a rope from up above to hang onto while they lowered the water. Then down went the water and they opened the other gates up, and out the other end I went. And, by golly, I had my first locks behind me. (laughter) The lock master was real nice. Asked me where I'd come from and where I was goin' and all of that, you know. And I felt real good about that. And glad to have that big worry behind me.

Because, you see, nobody was helping me. The whole trip I'd planned by myself. I financed it by myself. I arranged everything by myself. Basically, everybody was against it. And the only reason they let me was because . . . first of all, nobody was gonna *stop* me. Literally or actually. Besides, they thought I was gonna get out on that river, and after a while I was gonna head back for home. But I wasn't that kind of a guy. When I started something, I would stay with it; I never thought of quittin'. It just never dawned on me that there was such a thing as quittin'. And another thing, it was a family tradition; a Kurtz never quits. (laughter) So, once I started it, it had to be finished. No matter what came up, I had to figure my way through it and accomplish what I'd set out to do. Okay.

Now, there was another thing that was something to be real

concerned about. And it wasn't too far ahead. You get down to Red Wing, Minnesota, and Red Wing is a pottery center. There's a state penitentiary there too. And, uh, you know there's a little song about Red Wing. It's an Indian song that I grew up hearing. It's a very pretty song. (laughter) But anyhow, I stopped at Red Wing and I climbed Barnes Bluff—that's a bluff that's a *long* way above the river. You get clear on top of that and you're *way* up there on a little baby mountain, see. And you can look all over the country. You can look up the river. You can look down the river. And I looked down the river and I could see great big old Lake Pepin. And that's what had me concerned.

Lake Pepin was about, roughly, thirty miles long and three miles across. And it's boomerang-shaped. And there's a point on the inside of the boomerang that the Indians called Point No-Point. Because, when you're going around the point, you never see a point. But yet you can't look ahead around it and you can't look back around it. See what I mean? (laughter) Just a huge bend in the lake. Well, anyway. I had to navigate Lake Pepin. I knew there wasn't going to be any current in that. And I had to have wind fairly decent to get me down that thirty miles of lake. So—I got out in Lake Pepin sometime in the afternoon— that was a Friday—and the wind quit blowin' and, by golly, I was adrift. Just becalmed, so to speak.

Well, I was sitting out there. And I wasn't moving. Water all around me. And I'm saying to myself, I'm not gonna get to my destination this way. So, I had a single oar, and I took my rudder out and stuck this oar out the back. That's what you call sculling. You'd take a stroke from each side with one oar. And you'd manipulate your boat that way. You put in a lot of effort for what you gain. But, it's a means to an end. So I sculled my way across Lake Pepin from Point No-Point to a little lake town called Maiden Rock. Now that's an Indian name. It's named after an Indian love story, where an Indian maiden jumped off the rock, committed suicide, because she couldn't marry her choice, or something. And so they called it Maiden Rock. Anyhow, I spent the night there, and the next day I stayed in along the shore, and one way or another I made it to Lake City Port.

Now that's a big summer resort that's on a point out into the lake. It's called Lake City Port and it's owned by the city of Lake City. I wound up coming in there sometime that Saturday afternoon, or whatever it was. Yeah, Saturday afternoon. And I pulled up into the harbor,

or a big bay, on the down-lake side. Still no wind. No current. Still had half the lake to navigate, and I'd had a dickens of a time getting as far as I'd got.

Well, I woke up Sunday morning and what do you know! There I could see whitecaps on the water! And they were going in the direction I was going. And believe you me, I didn't waste any time. I got my sail up and I hustled out beyond that point and I picked up the wind and away I went. I didn't say good-bye to nobody or anything. I didn't even eat breakfast. And, hey, when I got out in that wind, I wished I'd stayed where I was at. Because I could see whitecaps, but when I got on 'em, and the farther down the lake I got, the *bigger* they got. Oh, they got monstrous. And, uh, my little old sailboat was just going wide open.

Well, I was looking around to see if I could see any other boats out there. And these great big old waves and these whitecaps snarling off the top of 'em. They would come higher than my boat, you know, and just look at me as they went by. And they didn't roll over because they would be thrown away from the boat by water action, see. When my boat would go down in a swell, she'd go clear down and a wave would just come up within inches from the back. And then she'd lift up and we'd ride the top of the swell and then we'd go down the other side headfirst and back up again. And I thought to myself, I made a lot of this stuff by myself. The rudder and the pin and stuff like that. And in order to take the rudder in and out, you had to turn the rudder all the way sideways. And I said to myself, now supposing my rudder busts. Or something happens to it. What am I gonna do? So I reached over between waves and I got my oar and I pulled it up to where I could get my hands on it real quick. I decided, you know, just how I was gonna manipulate everything. And I got everything lined up. And sure enough, it wasn't too long till my rudder pin broke.

Well—there I was, out in the middle of all that. And it wouldn't take nothing to capsize me if I went sideways. So I just did like I had figured it out. I just turned my rudder sideways and I caught her as the tail end went down and I turned that rudder over and pulled her out and stuck this oar in and brought her about and just kept right on a-goin'. And I noticed that there was cars stopping, up along the bluff roads. They have places for people to stop, tourists, where they can park and look out over the lake and picnic. And I noticed a whole bunch of cars stopping and people lining up along the bluff there, and I said, well what's wrong? Is there a boat in distress out here? So I raised up as high as I could and I looked in all directions and I wondered how I could help 'em if there was—I was having all I could do to take care of myself. But I couldn't see any boat or anything like that. And all of a sudden I said, hey, they must be looking at *me!* So I just took my one hand and I gave it a sweep in the air, and the minute I waved my hand, a whole sea of hands went up. (laughter) And I says, by golly, they are watching me! Anyhow, that's how I sailed my boat the last leg of Lake Pepin. Down to what they call Reed's Landing—that's where the lake goes back into the river.

Now there's a pontoon bridge across there, like in several places like that. And I pulled in that Reed's Landing to get my rudder fixed. And I heard somebody say, when I was in the restaurant there, they said, yeah, they'd heard on the radio that there was thirteen-foot waves on Lake Pepin today. So that's what I was riding down through Lake Pepin. Thirteen-foot waves! And I got smacked against the pontoon bridge before I got back in the river—the wind and the current was giving me such a hassle. But I finally got through there and back into the river and had my rudder going again and away I went. I went sailing down that river just lickety-splits. Went around one bend after another. But anyway, that was one of my first big adventures on the *early* leg of my trip.

III

Now, I want to say another word or two about locks before moving on. There's several locks on the Mississippi where you really have some heavy dropage. The Ford locks in Minneapolis—you have about a forty-foot drop. But I didn't go through that with a sailboat. I did go through it with the canoe. And then the Keokuk locks at Keokuk, Iowa. You have about a thirty-five-foot drop there. And that's just above the Des Moines River where, just below the locks there, you can look into three states. You can look into Iowa, Missouri and Illinois—where the Des Moines River and the Mississippi join. And then the Alton locks is about a forty-foot drop. The other locks drop different distances, but not near as much, see. These three locks are the main ones for heavy dropage.

Okay, and another thing. On my sailboat trip down the Mississippi, I saw some of these other locks in the process of building. Then when I went down two years later in the canoe, I locked through 'em. And I'd seen them in the process of building.

Now then. Coming to the mouth of the Missouri. I passed through the last of the dams on the river at Alton. Now that's a busy locks at Alton. My whistle sure didn't help me much there. And that lock master wasn't nothing like any of the rest of 'em. He was a mean, old, vicious, cussin', ornery cuss. You know what I mean. (laughter) He didn't have to be as ornery as he was. But he did have lots of traffic to take care of, lots of barges and things like that. And then me coming along with a little old sailboat. I wanted to get to the Missouri before

33

dark. I wanted to see it, and I wanted to navigate that fast water in daylight. Anyway, I got through there about sundown. And now I was gonna have to navigate ten miles downriver to St. Louis.

Well, I wasn't too good a navigator on the river at night, with running lights and buoys and stuff. And I had some pretty strict rules I stuck by. One of 'em is that you don't navigate on the river at night if there's waves. Because you can't hear the ripple of the water on your buoys. These buoys, you see, are out there for marking the channel starboard and port and so forth. And they're about as big as my boat. When they go wheeling around in the current, they're just not something that you want to get tangled up with. But mostly, you could get into snags or something like that, closer in to shore. And you don't know where you're at because when it's dark, it's dark. So, I would never navigate it unless I had a good moon and a quiet night.

And I used to really like to get out and drift with the current on those nights. It was beautiful out there. You could get away from the mosquitoes. You didn't have any head winds. The wind would drop at sundown. And you could just drift with the current. I'd run a kerosene lantern up my mast at night because no matter which way my boat turned, they'd be able to see the light. Kerosene lanterns burn good and they don't go out very easily. They didn't burn too bright, but out there on the river at night, why you could see it a long way off. So, that was safety, because a lot of times I would go to sleep on my sailboat, while I was drifting. (laughter) Now this is jumpin' ahead a little in the story, but . . . I remember one time I couldn't keep awake. Oh, I was fighting it and I was trying to make it to Caruthersville. I knew Caruthersville wasn't too far. And I was trying to make it there for the night. So I ran my lantern up my mast and I dropped off to sleep. I don't know what time it was at night, but the next morning I woke up and it was daylight. And my boat was on a mud bar and I didn't know where the dickens I was. As it turned out, I'd gone right down the river past Caruthersville, and the wind had blown me up on a mud bar just below there. So I never saw Caruthersville until I went down with the canoe a couple years later. But, hey, I've got to stop right here and tell you a story about Caruthersville. Now this is something you'll really enjoy.

Right after Pearl Harbor, I joined the Navy and I was going through boot camp at San Diego and I heard a couple guys talking there. One of them was an aviation machinist's mate. And it turned out that he had made two of the parts for Lindbergh's plane that flew the Atlantic. And the other one was a taxicab driver. They both came from St. Louis and so I told 'em about my trip down the Mississippi and then this one fella comes out with this story about Caruthersville.

One day, he says, he was walking up from the river to town. And, he says, there's a bunch of little old tarpaper shanties along on the right as you come up the slope. Well, he says, I saw this man, an old man, with a rake. He had his wife down and he was hackin' at her with a rake! Well, I went up to 'em, he says, and I took that rake and jerked it outa' his hands and threw it in one direction and slapped him down in the other. And, uh, the next thing I know, he says, she's got the rake and she's on *me* with that rake. And when I'm trying to protect myself from the rake, he gets something else and he's workin' on me from another direction. And by the time I got outa' there, he says, I didn't even have a shirt on! (laughter) And, he says, the people in town were all standing out in the street and laughing and having a big old time. Just laughing and laughing away. And they told him later that that goes on all the time. That old man and her are fighting like that all the time. But, boy, don't let anybody interfere!

Well, like I said, I'd slept through Caruthersville that first time down, but on the canoe trip I came through and I saw it. And hearing that sailor tell that story, I remembered seeing that old man, standing along there just gawky-eyed, you know. Just a hand-to-mouth existence. So I knew exactly what he was talking about. Okay, now. Another adventure that I had was on downriver.

Early on my trip I heard about these whirlpools and sucks in the river farther south. I was warned to watch out for 'em and so forth. I remember one was the Hickman Suck and another was the Osceola Suck. And then I knew there would be others, but I didn't know where. So, I kept that in the back of my mind. And that was another thing I had to be very concerned about. And I'm a very concerned person. I've got lots of nerve and everything, but I always like to keep things on the safe side. A calculated risk.

Now I like what President Lincoln said—no risk, no gain. But I've always kept the risks on a calculated basis, so if I missed, I would still have an out. Like for example, if I was trying to catch a freight train on the run, I'd run for the front of the boxcar. If I missed, I had the whole boxcar to push myself in the clear. I would never touch it on the back. *Never!* I wouldn't care what had happened; I wouldn't touch that boxcar in the back. Because that was no longer a calculated risk; that was a *dead* risk. And that's the way I operated my life.

Well, I kept my ears peeled and I asked people along the way and most of them didn't know anything about any sucks. These river people, if they live around something, they don't think nothing of it. And if they don't live around it, they don't know nothing about it. And so I remember coming down from St. Louis through the jetty country— I call it the jetty country because that's where they've tried to straighten out the Mississippi River by building jetties in to build up ground. And, hey, that water is fast; that's the fastest stretch of water on the whole Mississippi.

The Missouri comes in right above St. Louis ten miles and it pours down on you and then it narrows out. It goes between the bluffs on one side and then they try to jetty it on the other side to keep it in the channel. And to keep all that sand that comes down the Missouri River moving. Well, that's why they have these jetties, you know, and I tell you, when you go down through there, you want to know what you're doing. Because if you get in between one of those jetties, and that current would slap you up against the jetty, it would hold you there more so than if you was spiked to it. There's been people that in the dark got in there and it has dumped their boat against the jetty and they climbed the jetties and sat on top of 'em until they was rescued. And that water just held that boat until you couldn't get it out.

But, I was telling you, after I left the mouth of the Missouri, I started slipping downriver and it started getting dark. And the long and short of it was that I should have dropped anchor and spent the night and then come on down in the daytime. Because I was navigating that stretch of river at night, in that fast water. And, you know, normally they'd put a light on the end of a jetty. But here, instead of putting it on the *end* of the jetty, they've got the navigation light clear down on the *inside* of the jetty. Believe you me, if I would have followed that, I would have got in between the jetties and with that fast water I would have ended my trip right there. Just real quick. But I was, like I said, always real cautious. And not only that, but what really made it bad was the lights from St. Louis in the background just drowned out all of the navigation lights. And after a while I couldn't tell a navigation light from a street light.

36

But I wiggled my way on down until I got into St. Louis. And there's a big bridge across there and I went underneath that. I went underneath it on my port side and I found out later that there's a bar that comes clear up under that bridge, and if I'd gone out of the channel, I'd have wound up on that bar. I don't know what the repercussions would have been, but, anyway, I maneuvered into a marina and tied up. And the guy in charge let me sleep on one of the cruisers. So, it was nice to get into a good bed once in a while. And then the next day, I started on down the river.

Then, like I told you, I went through this jetty country, in fast water. And I remember a town called Chester, Illinois, and it's built right on the side of the bluff. I don't know how they could drive a car there. It's nothing but hill. Everything up and down. But, then, I came down from Chester, down to the mouth of the Ohio, where the Mississippi and the Ohio join. Well now, there again was some more things I was wondering about. Because I'd heard about where the two rivers come together.

Here's the black old water of the Mississippi and it comes to the light sandy water of the Ohio. And the two of 'em run side by side for miles. They slowly eddy together. The Mississippi's black water, the Ohio's sandy water. It's quite a long ways across where the two of them join. And I started going right on downstream and watching the waters mix. Finally the Ohio water swallows up the Mississippi water and it all becomes sandy.

Now I'm out of the Mississippi River, the characteristic river where the land comes down to the shorelines, so to speak. The way it does up above St. Louis. Up there you could pull over to the foot of the bluffs. And civilization would come to the river. There was stretches where it was wide open, and a lot of civilization from the mouth of the Missouri on up. But now I'm down into sandbar country. And as you go down the river, that Ohio and Mississippi comin' together, they really tear that river up for a ways, see. It comes down—I don't know how many miles—and makes a ninety degree turn, almost, to the left, or port. And, uh, then it heads on downstream.

I stopped somewhere, I don't know, that same afternoon, to mail a post card at a place where a slope comes down through the bluffs and there was a beach. Where the fishermen kept their boats. And a bunch of young men had congregated and taken their dip. And they were getting ready to go home. It was just before sundown. And I remember giving this boy . . . I wrote a post card home every day telling where I was and stuff, and I'd give it to somebody to mail. A fisherman on the river or whoever, it didn't matter. It always got mailed. Every single post card that I ever handed out was mailed. So I gave my post card to this boy as he was heading back through this cavity in the bluff toward town. It was called Columbus—that was the name of the town. And nobody said a word to me about nothin', and I just left Columbus and went on down the river.

Now, there was something starting to get a little fishy. You know, by now I had a built-in suspicion. Or instinct. And, uh, I didn't like something. I didn't know what I didn't like, but there was something I didn't like. And I kept watching the river and studying everything, the current, you know, and the surface. The action of the current on the water. And my subconscious mind kept telling me there's something wrong. Just watch yourself. So I'm drifting downriver and I come past a point. Now normally the water coming downriver will come to a point, and it ricochets away from the point into the current. But—this didn't do that. There was a great big bluff off to my left, sitting in a big pocket of water. And the river went on past the tip of that bluff. But when I passed this point I'm talking about, all at once the current made a left-hand turn, a port turn, without there being any shoreline. It just turned. And headed right for the bank while the river went straight! See what I'm talking about? My little old hair started to tingle and I says, there's gotta be something wrong now. Here I am, headed for the edge of this . . . you might say kind of a lake, off to the side and ahead, with a chalky-colored bluff down at the end.

So, it heads off port and it's picking up speed now and the undercurrent is just a-boiling. And then as it hits the bank, it turns and starts going down the bank. Well, now I'm clear off the channel, according to looks. And I'm going along and the water's just a-boiling and getting worse as it goes. When you get into boiling water, you don't necessarily travel faster, but the water is just a turmoil. It'll sometimes blow itself right outa' the surface—it'll go PPPSSSSSSS, you know. Now all that's coming up around my boat. And it's getting dark and I want to get off that river. And here I am in a pickle. And as I get down there farther, it gets worse.

Just about dusk I get opposite this big bluff. And this bluff is shaped like a fishhook. The shoreline comes down and goes into the bluff and fishhooks coming back upstream and out on a shallow bend. You see the picture? Now, I raised up on the seat of my sailboat, and I looked over in that hook—there was just enough light to see—and what do you know, here's a great big old whirlpool! And it's turning around, real sluggish. And inside, it was full of logs and sticks and all kinds of rubbish and debris. And it was turning around and around, no hurry at all. But a great *big* one. And she had some slope to her. So I wiggled along and wiggled around and made my way past her. And I thought, ahhh, I got clear of that. But the water that I was riding flowed down in there, some of it causing this whirlpool, and a lot of it coming out above the whirlpool. Because the channel was evidently deeper out there. And it took this current—now we're talking about the Mississippi and the Ohio current—it took this and whipped it right back upstream when it came around that fishhook. It threw it into the current coming down. And, hey, that water went into a hemorrhage. It started really cuttin' corners, see. It was just blowing up and boiling and snortin'. And you could hear it go sluuuuuuuuuup and stuff like that, you know.

Well, I was slipping out at the tip of the fishhook with my sailboat, and I heard all this noise and I think, ahhh, I'm just about back in the channel. I'm gonna be in the clear. But about the time I said that, why, a great big old whirlpool just all of a sudden developed. Right next to me. And I mean it was big. I'm talking not near as big as the one back in the hook but maybe thirty foot across. And it had a steep slope to it. It developed real fast and you could hear the old hole in the center go sluuuup sluuuup sluuuup. And, man, my hair liked to have pushed my scout hat right off. I didn't have time to think really. My boat started going right into it. It went around, and as it went around, it worked toward that hole, that suck in the center. And, boy, I thought, I'm gonna have to get outa' here. I grabbed my oar and I gave it a pull. Dug it in and pulled real hard, and I fell almost clear back off my seat. What had happened was I'd pulled with the current, and the current was going so fast I didn't have nothin' to pull against. And then when I turned around and dug it in the other way, it was just like digging it into solid ground. So I started pulling on that and it sucked me clear into the hole. And I felt my boat go sluuuup, sluuuup, you know, and it chomped it down. And, uh, then it made a second sluuuup, and I felt it go some more. And I looked back over the stern and there was about,

oh, maybe a couple of inches to the water. And I was thinkin', well, now what, you know. (laughter) But—after I plugged the hole with my boat, by that time, the whirlpool was playing out. See, they'll break in full force and then they'll play themselves out and close up, the water churn around and kill 'em. So then she spit me up, by golly. And I pulled on out into the channel. And I cleared the point.

Well, I got going downriver pretty good, the sun was just about over the treetops, and I saw a fisherman on the bank underneath the bluff. He was untangling some nets. And so I says to him real calmlike, I says, say mister, what was that I just went through? Oh, he says, that was the Chalk Cliff Suck. Well, hey, my old hair stood up good and proper then. So I says to him real calm, like so what, you know, I says, ever take any boats down? Oh, he says, thirteen or fourteen boats and a sea plane. (laughter) He kept right on untangling his nets and I said thank you and I went right on down the river. Now, I says to myself, this calls for a choice supper. So I broke out a can of Van Camp's pork and beans. And out of all the pork and beans I ever ate in my life, I never found a can of Van Camp's, or anybody's pork and beans, that ever had two pieces of pork in it! But that can did! (laughter)

So now I'm caught out on the river—I didn't get to shore fast enough. Evidently there wasn't no sandbar there or something like that because of the way the channel was running, and so I'm stuck out there after dark on a pitch black night just after I'd went through all of this stuff. I'm down below the mouth of the Ohio where the river is running fast and I'm heading straight for Hickman, Kentucky. Ten miles, I think it is, and there's supposed to be a suck called the Hickman Suck, right opposite Hickman. And I'm caught out on the river and I can't get off. Can't hardly see. Tryin' to keep in the channel. And I remember one thing I heard as I was going down that river, pitch black of the night. I heard somebody thumping away on a banjo back in the woods. I can still hear that yet. And I thought, boy, I'd sure like to be with him. Instead of out here, on this river. But I made my way on down to Hickman without any further calamity, and I docked at Hickman on the channel side. I don't know where the suck was, but I sure wasn't going to worry about that until morning.

IV

So, anyway, from Hickman, Kentucky, I left the next day. Now Hickman, by the way, is where—what's this old railroader's . . . train engineer's name? Casey Jones. Casey Jones is buried there. And—still on the subject of sucks—the Osceola Suck was several days south from Hickman. I figured I knew just about where it was located. So I started sidestepping it a long, long way before I got there. Instead of going down the channel side of the river, I stuck clear over in the dead water on the starboard side. And I went clear down, I don't know how many miles, just poking along, out of the wind and out of the current, until I finally got around the Osceola Suck—or where it was supposed to be. I don't know what it looked like. I didn't care. I'd had enough with the Chalk Cliff Suck; that had about scared the wits outa' me. Then I got back in the channel and headed on.

But, getting back to the Hickman area. Now I'm in a new type of river. Now we have sandbars. And they're nice. When you get out of the channel, you can get out of your boat sometimes a quarter of mile from the water's edge, and you can wade on the nice, beautiful, lovely, charming sand in the cool water. And it's fairly clear because it's dead water there and the sediment drops out of it, and it's just moving enough to keep it from being stagnant and not fast enough to have a lot of sediment. And you can walk in that on up to the beach, and you can go ahead and make a camp there at night if you want to and sleep on the sand. And you're far enough out from the shoreline so that you're beyond the mosquitoes. See, your tree line drops and then your shrub line, you know, bush line, and then your willow line, and it just fades right on out into the sandbar. And you can pull up there at night in the cool of the evening and take yourself a swim and cook yourself a meal and relax. Then wait for the moon to come up, sun to go down, and the wind to drop, and if everything is right you can push out again and navigate all night long.

So—after the river makes this one bend to the right, they're starting to riprap the river. That's something not new, but they're doing it in a different way. Up north, they would take barge loads of rock that they'd blast out of these cliffs—it's a kind of a limestone rock—and they would lay it on the bank. Up above the waterline. In layers. And then they would drop it on down into the water. So when the current would hit the bank, you see, it couldn't erode the bank away. The water would strain itself through these rock and leave sediments in some places and build up, and it would sweep 'em away in other places. But it would save that shoreline.

Now down south, right after I left Hickman, they had a different situation, They would have barges in the river and cables coming out from the bank. And they would put a willow foundation on and then they had these concrete pieces that had been made special for this with eyelets of cable sticking out of them. And they would interweave these cables with more cables and hook them all up together, the ones on the side and the ones up above—they was anchored to the bank, you see. And as they came out in the river, they just lowered them from the barges as they kept fastening them, and they could drop 'em clear down to the bottom of the river. So that way the current couldn't undercut the bank. That was something new they were doing in that stretch of the river, trying to keep the river contained in its channel by using these concrete aprons.

So, I saw my first ones on the first bend after I left Hickman. The current changes and goes on across the river—it doesn't just go straight across but rather it *eases* its way across. See, when it goes around one bend, it'll follow it and just ease its way away, and then it'll cross the river and finally hit the other side. All right, when it hits the other side, it starts going around that bend and *that's* where they've got to riprap the shoreline.

But, anyhow, this one particular bend that I want to tell you about they call the New Madrid Bend. After you make the second bend, you start swinging back to your left again, and you are going around a bend that is forty-two miles around. And two miles across. And one steamboat going upstream and another one going downstream are both traveling in the same direction. I would see the smoke from some of these coal-fired steamboats drifting across the peninsula, or this bend, hours before I'd run into the boat. And what was ironical and really upset me was how the wind behaved in there. I'd say, well, I'm buckin' the wind on this side, so when I get on the other side, I'm gonna have a nice tail wind. So I would buck the wind, drift with the current and make the bend, and I'd start down the other side—and here's that same wind blowin' upstream! It would get in between the trees on the bank, you know, and follow upstream just like the current would follow the river channel downstream. (laughter) It was cruel. Anyway, I went all the way around that bend and I wound up at New Madrid that night, at a sawmill. And that's where I camped.

V

Well, let's see. Moving along now. I was drifting down one afternoon—about ninety miles above Memphis, by river miles. Had sandbar to one side and caving banks and tangled trees to the other side, and, uh, stripped to my waist as I always was. No wind. I was just keepin' my sailboat in the channel and coasting with the current. And I noticed some buzzards sitting on some deadfall. And I was wondering why those buzzards was there. But when I got up a little closer, why, I noticed that there was a dead horse snagged in the dead trees and under-brush. So, by golly, I thought I'd shoot myself a couple old buzzards. Now I loved nature and I was a conservationist and there's a lot of things I wouldn't shoot. But I didn't see anything wrong about shooting some buzzards. At least, I'd never shot any and I thought I'd like to go home and say I'd shot a couple buzzards.

Well, I was looking down the sights of my .22 rifle at 'em. And it didn't seem to bother them any. They was looking at the dead horse with one eye and me with the other eye and waiting for the horse to ripen up a little bit so they could start their feast. So I started pulling the trigger on my .22, and you could hear the crack of the rifle echoing down the river for a ways. And the buzzards would just fluff their old wings out, just puff out and shrink back again. All they are is a big bunch of feathers with a little wick of a body that runs from the tip of their beak down to the tip of their toes. Well, I banged away and banged away at those rascals until I was clear outa' range. And I was shooting right through those feathers and I wasn't even shooting any feathers off! And I imagine those buzzards was just laughin' up their sleeve at me.

45

So, I put my rifle back and I got down to the next bend, which, I'll just say, swung to the right. And here, all at once, comes a skiff from, what looked like, right outa' the bank. Almost as if it came outa' nowhere, you know. Like it just appeared, how would you say, like some phantom. Now, from the position I was at, why, that's what it looked like. But what it really was was the mouth of a river, the middle fork of Forked Deer River. And this skiff had come out of the middle fork where the banks came right up to the river mouth.

Well, sitting back in the stern was this little old-timer. A red-headed, light-complected fella . . . looked like an Irishman. And rowing the skiff was a great big strapping Negro man. I remember how, just as clearly as if it happened yesterday, his shirt was torn, and his big black bulging muscles were pushing out through the rips. And this little older man calls out to me and asks me a few questions about where I'm coming from and where I'm going to and so forth. So I told him I was making a trip down the Mississippi River. And he says to me, he says, uh, why don't you stop and camp and fish and hunt with me for a couple or three days?

Now, I thought a minute and I looked at that big strapping Negro man and then back at the little old Irishman. And I thought to myself, you know, I'd been reading stories about this Mississippi River. I heard about how in the olden days they would lure people out into the woods and murder 'em and take their stuff and everything. Just made a game out of it, see. You have to consider that I was nineteen years old, and I hadn't been too far from home before that time, nor gone too long. And a lot of the stuff I knew about the South came outa' books. And some of those books were pretty old. So, I thought, hey, maybe they're gonna waylay me. But I remember sayin' to the man, I says, do you mean it? He says, of course I mean it. But, he says, you'll have to make up your mind real quick because if you get down below that little point sticking out of the bank, he says, you won't be able to make it back up again. So I decided, well, I'm an adventurer. And I'm a person that takes calculated risks. Okay.

I tried to make it back up, but the current was too fast, and I had no auxiliary engine—just me, I was the auxiliary. So I jumped out of the boat and grabbed the log chain that I had fastened to the end of the bow, and when I jumped out—right next to shore—I went down up to my armpits. And the ledges were clay and tough to get a hold on.

But I got my boat under control and then I gradually, by digging into the bank with my hands and feet, why, I worked my way back up to the mouth of the river and on into the river—up the mouth of the middle fork of the river.

Well, there was no current in there and it had big old garfish jumping around, and kind of a brackish-colored water, and the sun was hitting it from one side and it was kind of shady and overcast. The whole thing gave you sort of a feeling of being away from it all. You could be about anywhere in the world. Just isolated, so to speak.

So, I tied my boat up to the bank, and now I'm soakin' wet. And I wrung my handkerchief out, and then I took my .38 pistol and stuck it in my back pocket and poked my handkerchief down over it. And I figured, well now, if anything gets to be a little uncertain, why, I can always pull my handkerchief out to blow my nose. 'Cause my handkerchief would automatically turn into a .38 pistol, and, uh, I didn't have any qualms about protecting myself.

I went up there, and this big black fella was sitting on a little old stool. And this other older man came up and welcomed me and introduced himself. And we visited a little bit and then the Negro man said he had to start for home. And the other fella coaxed him to stay a little longer, but he said no. He wanted to get on home before dark because when he went through the woods there was water moccasins and cottonmouths. And he didn't want to travel at night—he was barefooted. So, after he took off through the woods—and that was the last time I saw him—I got a little more comfortable. I thought, well, now I'm only outnumbered equally. One-to-one. (laughter)

And so, we started visiting a little more and one thing led to another. And I wound up staying there for a couple or three days—I don't remember exactly. I'd have to look at my logbook. But he showed me he made his own furniture by hand, and he even had his own broom that he made by hand. He'd take a willow stick and peel the bark down, and not cut it off but just keep peeling it down. And he'd wrap the end of it with some more bark and tie it up, and here he had a willow broom. Now, his kitchen floor consisted of the ground. His shanty was sitting up on poles so that when high-water came all the way up the steep bank that I'd climbed to the top, and up through these poles, he would still be dry on top. And if he wasn't, well, he had a boat that he could get into. And everything that he probably owned in the world he

could put in that boat. And go to high ground until the water went down.

Well, he said he'd fix something to eat. Now back in those days, you know, people was very poor and food was not too plentiful amongst the poor. And me sailing along on a sailboat—I had to cook on sandbars if I wanted something hot to eat. And here, he invites me for supper. And I thought, hey now, that's all right. I can go for that. So he whipped up a batch of what they call shortening bread. You've heard that song about mama's little baby loves shortening bread. Those old-timers, hey, they could make the best shortening bread in the shortest period of time. Why, my word, somebody today showing you how couldn't even come close to them. What they would do is they would mix up some flour and water and put some shortening in it and some . . . ah, I forget what they used to make it rise. And they mixed that up and dumped it in a frying pan on a hot barrel stove and "bingo!" that thing would rise up like a mushroom and the next thing you know, why, it was done and you had hot shortening bread.

So—we had shortening bread and I don't know what else. And then it started gettin' a little dark, so we settled down for the evening and I brought my blankets up and we climbed the ladder into the loft. And that's where we slept at night. Up there it was just a little bit higher above the mosquitoes. Back in those days we didn't really have mosquito repellent. And, hey, I'm telling you, those mosquitoes had a field day. I'll bet the old mosquitoes told the young mosquitoes what a good, great time they had back in the old days before the repellent came along. Because, boy, I could tell you some stories . . . like for instance, back at the resort in Minnesota, there was this fella tellin' stories about mosquitoes.

Now, he says, one time he was out in the woods and he heard a racket. And he looked around, and, he says, he thought it was a B-17, flying treetop level. But instead, he says, it was two mosquitoes flying side by side. And they had their beaks underneath the armpits of a man, one beak under each side. And they came down and landed not too far from where he was hiding. By this time he really crawled into the smallest place he could get. And, he says, those mosquitoes was talkin', and one of 'em says, ahhh, let's eat this guy up right here. But the other mosquito says, no, let's take 'm back to camp and eat 'm in comfort and make those other guys back there jealous. And then the other mosquito says, nope, he says, I'm for eating him right here. Because if we take 'm back to camp, he says, those big guys back there are gonna take him away from us. (laughter) And that's just about the way some of those mosquitoes felt! The farther south you got, the bigger they got. Down there there's some hybrid mosquitoes they call saltwater mosquitoes.

Well, anyway, they ate so much of me that I don't know how I ever got to my destination in one piece. Because they started eating on me upstream and they just got fatter as they went. In the morning, sometimes, I would look at those mosquitoes that had feasted on me during the night. They would be on the boom of my sailboat. And they were so heavy with blood—you could just see the blood bloating 'em out like a balloon—so heavy they couldn't fly. They'd just made it over to the place on the boom, and if they'd ever got any farther out, they'd have fallen in the river and drowned. But, anyhow, like I say, the mosquitoes had a field day. And you just learned to sleep with 'em. You'd try to go to sleep real fast so that you'd be asleep before they started torturing you. And then wake up in the morning.

Well, okay. This old-timer and I got fairly comfortable with one another. I got to feel like I didn't have to worry about him waylaying me anyway. So we loosened up and got to talking. And I'd studied a little astronomy and a little archaeology, and I knew quite a bit about ornithology. And he'd ask me questions about these things. Indian mounds and such things as that, you know. I could give him some basic information. Well, one day I heard him talking to a neighbor that came by, and, uh, he was tellin' him what a smart boy I was. Man, he was really bragging me up. You'd think I was some Pulitzer Prize winner, or something like that. And I thought, my word. Was he trying just to be nice, or did he really believe it? But the short of it was he really believed it. And that rascal would keep me awake at night—I'd be so tired, and I'd wake up and answer his questions and go back to sleep and wake up again. And answer some more. (laughter) And he didn't even know I was sleeping, see. He just liked to talk and ask questions, and he was having a big old time.

Now this old fella's name was Mister Hammer. And he told me a number of things about his life that was real interesting. One thing was that he educated himself. And he could read the Bible. He had taught himself to read. And to write. And he had a beautiful handwriting. Man, his handwriting was just like artwork.

And I remember one time we went hunting together. There was these fox squirrels that would come out right next to the cabin in these trees, and we thought we'd try to get one for our meal. One or two. But, boy, they were really slick. They were smart. They would come out and tease you, see. And then the minute you picked your rifle up, they were gone! So, I slipped in a position where I could shoot through a crack in the wall—from the inside downstairs. And one of 'em came out and started teasing around and so I dropped him. But, wouldn't you know, he fell into a mess of nettles. Now, if you don't know what nettles are, they call 'em burn weeds. They grow high—these nettles were over our heads. And I ran in there looking for the fox squirrel. Couldn't find the fox squirrel, but the nettles sure found me. I was bare to my waist. And, boy, did they sting me!. Well, the way you handle nettles is you just go down to the river bank and get a bunch of nice, fresh, wet clay and rub it all over yourself. That wet clay takes the sting right out and after it's gone, why, you go wash the clay off and you're ready to go again.

Well, anyway, I never did get to eat one of those fox squirrels. But the old-timer took me back in the woods, and, hey, those trees were just huge. And he had located a number of bee trees, and he showed me three different ones. But one of 'em was in a honey locust, and it was a good thirty foot up to the first limb. And you could look up there into the sunlight and you see the bees just swarming over this big limb. The limb was as big as the tree itself. And he asked me how I'd go about getting the honey outa' that tree. Now that's what he lived off of—fish, game, honey and wild fruit.

But there was lots of different ways that these river folk made their living, so to speak. And each one of 'em had certain little quirks. Some of 'em trained hunting dogs and were guides for hunters in the fall and afterward sold their dogs. Some of 'em went rafting down the river and cut the logs outa' all the timber that slid over the bank. They'd cut them out and make them into rafts and float them down the river to a sawmill. But we're talking about *poor* people, and, uh, uneducated. But just real nice. I mean, once you got to know 'em, they were simply first class. That's all there was to it. I just wish I'd recognized then more the things I recognize now, later on in life, because I could have enjoyed them even more and enjoyed the trip even more.

But—getting back to this old-timer. He was tellin' me some stories of his life and about when he was bootlegging. I think he said he had about fourteen children, and his wife had run off on him. There was always other men and things like that, and then she'd come back home, and he'd take her back. And then she'd take off again and so forth. Well, anyway, he made his living bootlegging, and he had a still back in the woods a ways from the house.

Now he said there was a big old snake that started coming up every day at a certain time, and it would lay its head up on this big old stump and make some funny noises. And he described the snake to me and it was a good-sized rascal. Probably big enough to swallow a rabbit. So one day, he says, he was gonna take the shotgun down and blow the snake's head off. But, he says, I forgot that day. And the next day, he says, I was already started when I remembered my shotgun, and, he says, I started back to get it and then decided not to. And that, he says, was real fortunate that I hadn't. Because when he got to the still that day and started running things, why, the revenuers overrun 'em and got him. His wife had reported him to get him outa' her way. And she had built him up to the revenuers to be a real dangerous person. And if he had taken the shotgun down to his still that day, it's hard tellin' what might have happened. At least, if they had found a gun in the area, they would really have gone tough with him. They'd have thrown the book at him. But when she'd painted him up to be such a dangerous person, and then he didn't even have a weapon around, why, that put a different slant on things.

So—he said they threw him in the county jail at Ripley, Tennessee, and he was there for quite a while. I forget how long he said. Anyway, while he was there, he wrote a song about his life. And he said he gave the original copy to the sheriff's daughter—and, by golly, he gave me the second original copy. Now it was written about his wife, and it got into the hands of—through the sheriff's daughter—the hands of somebody on radio, and it was rewritten a little and put to music. And it became a hit song during that time. And anybody from back in the thirties would remember it—the title was "Oh Darling, You Can't Love But One." And I had the second original copy, but it disappeared when I went off to World War Two. Everything was stored away in the attic, and the summer resort in Minnesota was semi-abandoned for a number of years. And the mice got in and ate up a lot of paperwork, and I think that's one of the things they got. But I do still have the old gourd drinking dipper he gave me. I do still have that.

So, uh, he was on the chain gang there. And they kept throwing hints at 'm, you know, that he should take off and go. They couldn't pardon him. But they didn't want to keep him. They knew he was kind of a harmless sort of guy. And they wanted him to go. So, he says, one day I went for a drink of water, he says, and after I took my drink of water, I just kept right on walkin'. He just walked on home, and they never came looking for him anymore. And that's where I found him when I came down the river.

Now another story that he told me was about when he was younger, and he was out hunting with his son. They came upon a neighbor man and his son. They were on the side of a hill and it was rocky. And I don't know what the trouble was about. But, anyhow, he had on one of those heavy felt hats, and in the course of things this neighbor flew into a rage and swung his axe at him. Now it was a single-bit axe and he was swinging on 'm with the back of it. And it hit the side of his head and that heavy felt hat caused it to glance off. And he said that it knocked him down, but, he says, I hung onto my gun. It was almost like self-preservation, you know; you don't let go of your weapon. And, he says, I had both hands on my gun. One of 'em was across the barrel and the other one around by the trigger mechanism. I would try to get up, and I could see the man running away from me. It was kind of in a swirl. And I'd fall down, he says, and the rocks were tearing up my knuckles and the skin off my fingers and my hand. And I rose and fell three times before things cleared up enough that I could get aim. And, he says, I shot the guy. And killed 'm.

Now there was nothing wrong with him killin' the guy except that he shot 'm in the back! And that's where he got in trouble. So, they put him in prison for shooting this man because it was no longer self-defense. The guy was running away and had his back turned. But, if the man had been facing him, why, nobody would have said a word. Anyway, he told me this when we were up there trying to sleep one night. He just up and says, you know, one time I killed a man. And there we were, in back of this little old stilt cabin, clear back in the woods at night while I was swatting mosquitoes, and he tells me that, a nineteen-year-old kid. (laughter) Well, I tell you, my hair perked up as well as my ears. But that was the life of some of these river people.

VI

Now then, I come on down to Memphis and . . . as you're coming down to Memphis, the river crosses from side to side about five times in just a short distance, maybe a couple of miles. And that's what they call Black Cat Crossing. I think it was mentioned in Mark Twain's writings. And then from there you can look on downriver and off to your right and you can see an old landmark looming in the distance called Walnut Bend. That's another landmark that's mentioned by Mark Twain in his writings. It's a long, long ways bluff to bluff now. That river will wander back and forth through ten miles of river-bottom. And I remember when I came by a couple years later in the canoe, I paddled over where there was solid ground two years before, now some of the wildest water on the river. (laughter) But, the river does change, and uh, it's quite a river.

Now, after you round the bend, after Black Cat Crossing, you could look downriver and you could see Memphis, twenty miles away, sitting on the bluffs like a kind of castle-city, like, you know, in a fairy tale. Up there in the beautiful, golden, sunlit sky—clear sky, hot, humid, but beautiful.

And you start drifting toward Memphis in becalmed waters and you go mile after mile and Memphis looks like it's running away from you like a mountain. But finally you get down to where you come to Memphis. And up the mouth of the Wolf River and up to a dock, and then you say, ummmm, ice cream. You lick your chompers and you head for town with a few little nickels in your pocket—remember, this is back in the days when times were tough. And five cents would buy a nice ice cream cone, and I don't mean any junky one. I'm talkin' about a *goooood* ice cream cone. A mouth-watering one. Anyway, you'd climb the old banks. Go into Memphis. And there you're swallowed up by a very beautiful southern town. Very nice, hospitable people.

Well, I'd head for a place where I could get myself some good ice cream and maybe a hamburger or something like that. Maybe I'd put a shirt on to go to town in, but I'd still be barefooted, or I might be wearing a pair of moccasins. And, so, when I left Memphis, I came down out of the Wolf River into the Mississippi, and I sailed for Helena, Arkansas. And I went at night because it would be cool, and the current is just as strong at night as it is in the daytime. And you don't have any upstream breezes blowing. So, I drifted all night under starlit sky. And some early time in the morning I rounded a bend and I saw a bunch of lights and I coasted into the beach of what is Helena, Arkansas.

Now, Helena, Arkansas, didn't mean anything in particular to me. But it turned out to be a town that had a lot of history in it. Some Civil War activities went on around there as they did in a lot of places up and down the river. And, uh, I made friends with a young man named Paul Malloy. His mother and him lived in a little old houseboat, or a kind of a little shanty, right down on the sands where the high water had drifted back into the channel and left some sand and debris. They were camped there. Paul and I got to be friends, and he ran around town with me, and he showed me different places. It was always nice when I went to a town to meet up with some young person my own age and run around and look things over. Maybe he'd show me a lot of out-of-the-way spots that an ordinary tourist wouldn't find.

Now Paul was uneducated, and it's interesting how a person without a day's education inside of a schoolhouse can explain things to you. How he would explain the war, and how he would explain historical things. I didn't know that he didn't have an education. And I didn't know sometimes what he was talking about, because if I'd known he didn't have an education, I coulda' put two and two together. (laughter) But under the circumstances I didn't always know what he was talking about. Anyway, he showed me around. And I decided I would go to church one night; he said there was some kind of a meeting down there. And I said I wanted to go someplace where they was friendly. I didn't know much about church or anything, but I thought I might meet some people. So he took me to a church.

And, say now, they were really on fire. That preacher, he preached for half an hour. And if you ever heard some of those old hillbilly, southern people talk, they got a language all of their own. You have to live with 'em awhile before you can understand it. It's English, but it's an English that you never heard before—and you'll probably never hear again. Because it came from a little locality or maybe a family or something like that. But he preached for about half an hour, and he was on fire from head to foot. And I never understood a word he said. Then when he finished, everybody just got up and walked out. And that was the end of that. I didn't find 'em very friendly, and I was a little disappointed because I wanted to meet some people.

Well, I got ready to leave Helena, Arkansas, and I headed on down the river from there, and I was down quite a few miles, and I saw where I could take a shortcut. Chop off a bend. So I pulled off the main channel and started workin' through this shortcut, and as I always found a shortcut, a shortcut turned out to be a longcut. When I got out of the channel, I got out of the current, and also out of the wind. And this current through the shortcut would be real slow. I just drifted, making feet instead of a good distance. I was creeping along through snags and things like that. And what happened on the other end is something I'll always remember.

When I came out of the—what we called a "cut"—and back into the river channel, I was at a ninety-degree angle to the main channel. And when I hit the channel, the biggest stern-wheel paddle on the river was going by. Mark Twain wrote about it. And it was still on the river, splashin' water and sinking skiffs and doing lots of other mischief up and down the river. She had a paddle wheel, a *big* one—in fact, from Mark Twain's day they had cut this paddle wheel down and made it smaller. But she was still the biggest on the river. And she was called the *Sprague*. She hauled the longest barge load in history. I forget how many barges she hauled down from someplace up the Ohio. They sunk some of the barges on the way down, but she still hauled the biggest load in history.

Well, she was going by, and I was coming out of the shoot, and I made the mistake of not waiting. I pulled right in behind the stern-wheeler as she went by. And, hey, I want to tell you something, that was a roller-coaster ride like you'd never forget. I picked up those roller-coaster waves. And I'd get up there with that little old sailboat, and she'd come to the top and that old mast of mine would go *swish* through the air, see. (laughter) And down the other side I would go. My heart would be up in my throat, and I'd think I was gonna hit the bottom of the river. And she'd get down there, and water would come right up to the side, and the old boat would rise up and straighten up again. Then she'd go up the other side of the trough and whip the mast across and down the other side. And, hey, my heart was jumpin' between my toes and my mouth. I didn't really know what was going on. I'd been on the river enough, but you don't see these same boats all the time. And sometimes that old *Sprague* passed me at night, see, when I was at anchorage. But, anyway, like I say, I was nineteen years old, and I had a lot to learn. And the *Sprague* was one of my teachers.

So, after she'd gone by and about swamped me, why, I come to a fisherman on the beach. He was working around his boat. So I decided I'd pull up and camp with him that night. And I did. Now as you climbed the bank from the riverbed up, each level that the Mississippi had stayed at for a certain length of time had cut a ledge, like a step. And the ledge would vary in height and depth depending on how long the river had stayed at one stage or how fast it had dropped. And these steps went all the way to the top of the bank.

When I got up to the top of the bank, there was a young fisher-man couple and an old fisherman couple up there. They had a camp made and they were fishing. So, I remember having a bite to eat with them, and then the young man went to visiting with me, and we sat along the bank overlooking the Mississippi River. It was a full-moonlit night, and we were sitting on these ledges, and I could sit on one ledge and put my arm on the other ledge almost with home comfort, see. The sand was always soft, and it got a little breezy out there, and the mosquitoes would stop. I was tired after a day on the river. Well, he went to talkin', and, hey, I wanted to listen to everything that guy said. Because here he was, another uneducated person that had never been to school. But, uh, what was ironic about it was that he had married a girl from Hannibal, Missouri, who was high school educated. And they was out making their living on that river. Now he's one of the ones that trained dogs and was a hunting guide and would raft logs. And he fished. But I was sittin' there just trying to keep awake, like I was up there in that old-timer's cabin back up the river. And I couldn't. I'd go to sleep and he'd be talking and I was saying "uh-huh" when I went to sleep. And I'd wake up and I'd see the moon had dropped some and he was still talking and I kept on saying "uh-huh." Everything he was saying was so interesting.

He was telling me about an old Civil War prison that was caving out of the banks where he got different things for weighting down his trout lines and sinking his shrimp boxes. Anyway, the next day he gave me a big old slave ball; I still have it today. And a foot scraper that you stick in the sand for cleaning the mud off your feet. I woke up once and heard him say, he says, ya see that sandbar over there? And he described it. And I says yep. And he says, there's a black fella buried over there. And, hey, that really woke me up. My eyes really popped open. And he says, I found 'm floating down the river. And he said he just drug him out and dug a hole in the sandbar and buried him. Never reported him. No more said about it. Wherever he came from—who knows? That was just his way of handling the situation.

Well, anyway, I remember when I came by there two years later, I stopped at the same place. The young couple was gone, but the old couple was still there. They'd built a tarpaper shack. Had a few chickens. And they was still campin' on the same spot.

VII

Well, here I am, cruising down the river on a nice, hot, sultry southern day, and it's getting along in the evening and the channel narrows out, considerably. Now I've got banks on *both* sides of the river. This is unusual. Usually a channel would be cutting away at one side and you'd have high banks there and on the other side you'd have sandbars. But now I'm traveling right straight between two banks. The channel is fairly narrow, and now it's starting to cool off because I kept getting in the shade, and dead ahead I see a bend. I'm gonna make a left-hand turn. And I'm about out of drinkin' water, so I'm gonna get a little water. And I wanted to find out too where I was at, and a few things like that.

So, I tied my sailboat up at the foot of some caving banks, and I started to climb the banks. Now it was just like climbing a baby mountain because the bank had caved into the river. And there was a fence down there and trees at all different levels and roots. And I would climb this way and pull myself up that way and I wiggled and squirmed and finally got to the top. On the downstream end. And I walked on up the back and as I got to the top of the bank, I see something that was very picturesque. There is a young lady with an old Dutch blue bonnet on just like you read about in stories from way back. And she's wearing a calico dress, a long calico dress, all nice and persnickety and pretty. Well, she's out there and her husband has just built a fire underneath a tub of water and he's getting it going and she's gonna do the washing.

Well, I got to talking with them. And it turned out they'd just gotten married. That was his bride. Get the picture? (laughter) Here

they are living in a little old shanty on top of this bluff and she's out there gonna do the washing in this Mother Hubbard's bonnet and this nice, blue calico. And she was so shy she could hardly look at me. I came up stripped to my waist and barefooted, you know. And her husband was chewing tobacco—he had a big wad tucked in his cheek. And he told me that where I'd just climbed up, there was three acres of land that had caved into the river all at once. It was just like a baby earthquake. And there was a sandbar across on the other side at that particular place—now I said I went down through narrows, but after I made that bend, it widened and opened out on the other side, see. He said there was a houseboat over there and the tidal wave just about swamped that houseboat. And other fishing camps along that bar.

Anyway, I said to 'm, how far is it to Vicksburg? Oh, he says, ten miles. I ain't never been there, he says, but it's ten miles. Come on, he says, and I'll show you. So we walked over to the edge of the caved bank and he pointed straight downriver and there was Vicksburg! Just like a fairy-tale city on the side of a hill, just settin' there in the afternoon with sunlight streaming all over it. He'd never been there, but he knew it was ten miles, and he pointed it out to me. He had ice water, too, and he said that was the end of the ice route. So they got ice every day. Well . . . you get the picture of the decor of the life that was going on at the time. And so I thanked 'em and I got my water and I edged back down the bank, got into my sailboat and went on down the river to Vicksburg.

When I got to Vicksburg, of course, I wanted to see the sights. Now remember I told you I started out with $11.05 in cash and then I had a supply of canned goods and food on my sailboat. Didn't have dehydrated food back in those days. They just had canned goods or stuff like oatmeal and Cream of Wheat. Hey, boy, you should know. Sometimes I ate three meals a day on Cream of Wheat. I'd make up one batch on a sandbar, you know. Cook it with driftwood and put it in these cake-tin plates that I had and then eat off of that as I went down the river. Get hungry, I'd just eat some more corn mush. Sometimes I had three meals a day of corn mush. I mean, this is the poor boy's way of travelin'. (laughter)

So, anyway, I got to Vicksburg and that meant maybe a hamburger or two. An ice cream cone. And I remember I tied my boat up to the bottom of a concrete apron that kept the current from washing, and I walked a long ways up from that—I don't know how far. And then I walked through gates between a concrete wall. It was just like walking into some kind of fortified city. They've got these flood walls around the city on the lower level, see. And then you continue to walk on up into town. Well, I headed for the first ice cream parlor I could find. And from there, then, I looked Vicksburg over. Now I don't remember too much about Vicksburg on the first trip, but when I came back in the canoe, we really looked Vicksburg over good. We met some young men and they took us around and showed us a lot of things. But I won't go into that right now.

I left Vicksburg at night so I wouldn't have to buck too heavy a wind. And I started drifting down for Natchez. Now Natchez is just loaded with history. You've got these big mansions and things like that, you know. They were building them right up to the time of the Civil War. Yeah, they've got tourists that go through there and hire guides to take 'em through and tell 'em everything. And they've got these old southern oaks that grow right down to the ground, their limbs dipping down and coming up again, and they're hanging with Spanish moss. For a kid from Minnesota, it was kind of like being in another world.

But, before we get to Natchez, after I left Vicksburg, I was drifting along down the river. And I got real tired and I hung a lantern up my mast. It wasn't too bad a night to be on the river. And I went to sleep, fighting as hard as I could to keep awake. I'd just dropped off when, all of a sudden, it was daylight! Hey, I came barreling out through that narrow cabin door of mine right into the glaring spotlight of a steamboat. A carbon arc light. And the minute I came out of the cabin, he took his light and whipped it over to the bank. Now, just to show you how these pilots operate. See, he woke me up with his light—he'd seen my lantern up my mast. And as soon as I came out of the cabin, he shot the light over to the bank to show me my location. Then as fast as he got me oriented that way, he shot it over the other side to show me the sandbar. Then he shut his light off. And immediately I took my boat and pulled it over to the sandbar and out of the way of the steamboat. It was the *Franklin D. Roosevelt*. A towboat. And I'd just cleared her nicely when she went on by, and on down around the bend, or through a shoot, or whatever, and I followed her.

Now, that morning I passed the mouth of the Black River and I saw my first Spanish moss hanging from the trees. And the sun come up and, oh, the thermometer on my cabin shot to 120°, psssho. Just like that, you know. And I've seen it go clear up to the top and mush out, where it couldn't go any further. So, uh, it was calm; there wasn't a whistle of wind blowing. And the sun was beating down. There wasn't no mercy. And I hadn't had my breakfast yet.

As I got to the next bend and it turned left, I got caught in a backwater. It was where you had your channel going downstream. And then there's a point sticks out up here into the channel and then down here there's another one. So in between them, the water, the outside current, doesn't get in and flow along the bank. There's just dead water in there. Now, when the outside current comes down, it starts an action—you know that law of physics that says for every action there's an equal and opposite reaction. Well, as it passes this dead water on the inside, it starts moving it in the opposite direction, just like a gear. So you got water going up one side and coming down the other, sitting in between these two points. I stopped to eat my breakfast, and I got caught in between these points. And I ended up heading back upstream!

I thought, well, there's no use going back upstream when I could be driftin' downstream. So I started to swing out of this backwater into the channel again, and as I was pullin' out, there was a towboat coming by. It was actually the same thing as the city of New York uses for their garbage boats to tow their barges out to sea. And it was hauling a string of pipeline barges. And as I was pulling out, they saw me and they noticed the name on my boat, you know. So they slowed up and signaled me to hook on. Hey, I thought, that was pretty nice! So I hooked on and then I walked up the string of barges, up to the boat, and, I'm telling you, that deck was so hot that it burned my feet right through my shoes. And you could have cooked an egg on it, had no trouble at all. But we'd stand up where the water would splash over the end of the barge and keep the barge cool. After a while they said they were gonna make tow with the *Tunica* a little farther down. They had a piece of dead water down there, off to the port side of the channel, and they pulled out there and made tow. And I went my way.

But, when they started down again, they slowed up for me to catch on. So I hooked on again—I thought that was great, with the heat and no wind and everything. I was gettin' a free ride. So I spent the day with them and we went right on downstream.

VIII

We passed Natchez. Just about sundown. And we was sup-
posed to pick up a tow with the *Mississippi*, the biggest government paddle wheeler on the river. We was supposed to pick it up above the
Glasscock shoot, ten miles below Natchez. They were gonna have to
break one tow and make another one just above the shoot because the
Tunica wasn't a powerful enough boat to take this load through the
shoot. It was a new shoot, and the water traveling through it was doing
about seven miles an hour. And that's galloping water because the normal current on the Mississippi is about three and a half miles an hour.
And when you start to double the normal current, I mean you've got
something like doubling fifty miles an hour to a hundred miles an hour
on a highway. It'd be about the same equivalent, see.

So, anyway, when they went to making tow, why, in the shuffle
at night, and the spotlights, and the one crew going off duty and the
other one coming on—it was just a hassle. And they apologized to me
later for the messy tow that they were making, but I didn't know what
they were doing. And while they were making tow, I thought they were
gonna sink my sailboat there for a minute because it got smashed in
between two barges and busted one of my windows out—in the Navy
they call 'em ports—and I almost broke tow to get myself in the clear.
But then everything straightened out. And after they got to moving
down through that shoot, I started walking up this string of pipeline
barges to the steamboat. It was at night, now, and there was heavy
smoke from the stack drifting out over everything, you know, as they

were running a heavy load of steam, and there was lights playin' from the steamboat on the barges and on the water. And it was cool, starting to get worth living again. And I was walking up toward the steamboat, gonna have the adventure of looking it over.

I came to a place where I just started to slip through the cables, along the deck. You know how they have these cable stringing from post to post. They're like guardrails, but they're not rails. They're flexible. And I started to slip through on the right side of a stanchion. I was almost through . . . now just follow this real close. I was almost through; it would have been easier to have continued than to back out and do what I did. But I looked, as I was going through, and I saw that the cables were a little lower on the left side of the stanchion. And I said to myself, hey, this has been a hot, hard day. There's simply no use exerting any more energy than I absolutely have to. I said that subconsciously, at least. I said, I'll just pull myself back and go in on the left side. And like I told you, the smoke and lights and the dark around these barges was all kind of blending together.

Well, I stepped back, and I made a step with my left foot so I could go in on the left side of the stanchion. And my left foot . . . never hit . . . nothin'! The end of one pipeline barge and the beginning of the other one was camouflaged together with the lights and smoke, and I wasn't looking that sharp, probably. I was only gonna step on the other side, just *one* step. And my foot hit nothin'. And, hey, in one flash I knew what had happened. In one flash the whole situation went through my mind. And I said, hey, this is it. I'm in trouble!

As my left foot went off the end of the barge, I shot my hands ahead 'cause I knew the other barge was out there. And I thought, if I could just stop myself, get a hold of anything so I could get a grip on something. So I shot my hands ahead for the next barge, and the tips of my fingers barely hit it, about numbed 'em. Whuuuuu, they just whipped by. And my left arm hit the water first. My head went under—I'm tellin' this in slow motion, see—and my scout hat was whipped off by the current. I still felt my right foot hanging on that barge up there. I'm gonna keep it there as long as I can. And now I'm down, my right arm's in, everything's in and my right foot leaves, and the barge sweeps over top of me.

Now, I'm trapped in the fastest water on the Mississippi River. Trapped between the bottom of the Mississippi and the bottom of these barges—they're going over the top of me. And there's a paddle wheel right down there not too far that I just got through looking at as I walked up. And they were turning that thing as fast as they could to get as much headway as they could with that load. Because when it got into that fast water, they had to have headway in order to control it. Otherwise, the current's the boss. See what I mean? Unless you're moving faster than the current, the current controls you. And I'd stood looking at that paddle wheel chunkin' and sploshin' with the spotlights on it, and I said to myself, man, I'd sure hate to go through that thing. And about a minute later, I was on my way.

So now, uh, I'm just a kid, nineteen years old. But, hey, I'm no dummy. I mean, I was naive in all kinds of things, but when it came to the out-of-doors and things like that, I knew my way around. And the minute I knew what was happening, I knew what I was gonna do. I headed straight for the bottom of the river. My aim was to get below that paddle wheel and come up behind it and then swim to the bank. Now I was a good swimmer; I was in good shape. And I wasn't a bit worried. All I wanted to do was clear that paddle wheel. I was thinking more about the embarrassment of the whole situation than I was about the danger at the time. And so I headed for the bottom of the river.

All the while I was calibrating in my mind how long it would take before I was clear of that paddle wheel. And when I'd hit that cool water after a hot day, it really stimulated me. It really put life into me, exactly like jumping into a cold shower. So I'm swimming for the bottom and timing it out. But I'm about out of breath. This all happened without me getting a chance to take a good breath, and I'm down there deep in the water. I could feel the water pressure and everything. And it's night, just pitch black. And now I'm in undercurrent too. I could feel myself being swished around by that about like a towel in a washing machine. But here, I was smart again. I says, okay, I'll save my energy. After I get down below the paddle wheel, I'll just completely relax and leave myself go. Save every ounce of energy I can. And that saved my life. 'Cause I was gonna need every ounce.

After I figured that I should come out about twenty feet beyond the paddle wheel—and I allowed plenty—I turned myself around and started swimming for the top. Wide open. And I was bustin' for air. Up I go, and then all at once . . . ka-bang! Something hits me, hard, above the left eye. And it just about knocks me out. And I almost let my breath out. I almost went unconscious. But that cold water stimulated me enough to keep me from doing it. And I locked my breath in, and about that time I got hit again, just below the left shoulder blade right at the base of my back. And for a second I thought I might have got clipped by a rudder on one of the barges beyond the paddle wheel—I was so sure I was clear of that paddle wheel. But I wasn't! And then I got hit again, right on the bottom of my left hip, and then again, right at the bottom of my left calf. Ka-bing-bang-bang-bang-powack, you know. And I felt myself really slushing around, like I was in a washing machine going full blast. But I hung onto my breath.

That current evidently took me down. The paddle wheel pushing against the river current, or the countercurrent, or what, but I felt myself go down deep because I could feel the pressure again. And, boy, when I came up that time, I *knew* I was clear of that paddle wheel. I came up, oh, I can feel the pressure letting off as I kept heading for the surface, just wide open, bustin' for air, couldn't get there fast enough. And when I broke the surface, I think I came out clear up to my waist. (laughter) Felt like it anyway. And, hey, man, I sounded like a big old snappin' turtle when I let my air out. Boy, it came out with a wheeeeeew! And I started suckin' in that old oxygen, and I wasn't worried about the river. I felt now I was safe, you know. It was just a matter of swimming ashore.

So, I caught my breath and treaded water a little bit. And I started. Well, I says, which is the closest shore! And the shore of Mississippi was closest. Here I am, going down the Mississippi; I go through the paddle wheel of the steamboat *Mississippi*; and now I'm swimming for the state of Mississippi. (laughter) So, I started swimming for the shoreline, and of course, all you see was shadows. Just the outline of the shoreline. And I started swimming for that, and, by golly, I couldn't keep my head above water! I was swimming wide open just to keep my head above water. And I wanted to get my shoes off—now I see I'm in a real pickle. So I wanted to get my shoes off so I could swim better, but I couldn't because the minute I stopped, I got sucked under by the undercurrent. And then I'd have to swim like the dickens to get to the top for some air again. And the minute I'd slow down swimming, why, the undercurrent would get me. So I wasn't going no place; I was just out there keepin' my head above water. I was swimming wide open, and I could only last a certain length of time doing that.

All right, I said, I can't make it to the shore of Mississippi, so I'll swim for Louisiana. And I head for Louisiana. But I see now, this is about the second time I'm down, and, boy, it took me some long, hard kicking to get up to the top again. And I knew I was about played out. And I knew my days were numbered.

Now, I'm telling you, this next thing was the most humbling experience of my life. Really it was. Well, one of the most humbling—I think the second most humbling. (laughter) Anyway, I hollered for help. And, oh, I sounded silly. Out there hollering for help. *Me!* I mean I couldn't get over that. I was proud, you know, a young kid. I was cocky. My brother always called me cocky, anyhow. And, uh, I *was* cocky. And here I am, hollering for help in the middle of the night, in the middle of the river, a good swimmer, hollering for help. I cupped my hands and kicked my feet and hollered HELLLLLP! And I drug it out. But I could see that old paddle wheel with its spotlights on it going down the river; it was quite a ways from me by this time. And, uh, I thought to myself, boy, it looks like this is the end of the road.

And, uh, so I went down another time. And I couldn't swim anymore. I mean, I didn't give up. Like I told you, we Kurtzes are fighters; we never give up, see. We never quit. But I'm down there and I need air and I don't have any strength left. It was right at that crucial time where I make up my mind which way I'm gonna go. Gonna let the air out and drown, or gonna fight. And I says, hey, I'm gonna fight until I pass out, and if I drown then, I won't have to be ashamed of myself. (laughter) And, boy, I turned everything loose, turned the old adrenalin loose, and, by golly, I cleared the surface. And, what do you know, I could see a spotlight coming back. And I could hear voices a ways down the river.

I could see the spotlight coming from what we called a gas boat. And that gas boat was coming back right up the path of the steamboat, and it was playing that spotlight on the water. Back and forth on the water. These are old rivermen; they know exactly what to do. They know exactly how to do it and everything, see. And so they was right on the ball. They played that spotlight back and forth, and here I am. The undercurrent now is holding me up! You see, instead of sucking me down, I'm in an area now where it's buoying me up. And so I'm suspended there waiting for that boat, and that spotlight's playing back and forth. There's a gap, you know, that it takes every time it comes forward. So I wait until it just comes right down, and I stick my hand up. And he hit it with the light and went on by and come back and locked in on my hand. Then he locked in on me. And he came by me, and I could see his face as they passed me.

They cut the engine. And the guy on the deck was untangling the rope from a life preserver. He was stepping in and out of it, you know. And he was a little ways away by that time and he says, here, son. Catch this! And he threw it at me. And he landed it right in front of me. Good thing it didn't hit me because I didn't have enough strength to do nothing anymore. That life preserver was about . . . oh, I would say, about two feet from me. I could see the rope playing out on the little gas boat. And I see that life preserver floatin' there. And I'm looking at that thing like a starving monkey looking at a banana. I can't even put my hand through it; I can't even reach out to get it. I was that weak. And I lay back in the water till the water filled my eyesockets, just my nose and mouth sticking out. Then I took a couple of deep breaths, and I came up real slow, straightened myself up, and I made one fast swish with my left arm. And I threw my right hand for the life preserver and just caught it with the tips of my fingers. I was afraid that they were going to jerk it away if they came to the end of the rope. And if they had, I couldn't have grabbed it again. So I held onto that life preserver with only the tips of my fingers and kept watching in the spotlight and seeing what was going on. Now all of this is happening real quick, see. I see what is happening, and I knew I had to make for it, and so I made a few fast kicks, and oooohhhh, I slipped my arm through it! And about that time, they come to the end of the rope.

Well, then they pulled me on in. And helped me onto the boat. And you know the best thing I could say about how I felt when I hit that deck? All the muscles in my body felt as loose as a ring of keys that you'd just shake and jiggle. It felt like you could blow wind right between my muscles, you know. I was just that loose. And, hey, those rivermen couldn't get over it. They couldn't get over it, no way. They took me back to the steamboat. Those guys, all that could get to see me, they stood and looked at me—and I can see 'em yet. They just looked at me like they was seein' something and they wasn't seein' it either. They shook their heads in amazement, and they simply could not get over it. Of course, I didn't understand the seriousness of the situation. I was embarrassed. Here I am, I'm *embarrassed.* (laughter)

And they're all looking at me like I'm real and not real.

Well, different ones told me stories. And I remember the Captain—Chautin was his name—he told me, he says, you're the eleventh man I've seen go overboard, and there wasn't any of 'em went overboard in worse water than you did. There wasn't any of 'em went through the paddle wheel. And there wasn't any of 'em went overboard at night. And most of these men, he says, never even surfaced once. They fell off the boat in broad daylight right when we were anchored, dredging. They went down and that was the end of 'em; we never saw 'em again until we picked up the body on a sandbar days later. And those guys couldn't believe it. Man, they just looked and looked at me.

But now I want to take you back a minute to when I started planning my trip, back in Minnesota. You know, I'd said to myself, it's logical that sooner or later I'm gonna run into a tight spot. I didn't know what it would be; I didn't know what that river was or nothin' about it. But, I says, there may come a time when I'm gonna have to battle for my life. So, I says, I got to get myself in perfect shape, then if an emergency comes up, I'll be able to meet it. I wanted that margin of error. So I would run from my house on the resort to the railroad tracks at Richmond, a little under two miles. Every day I'd jog up there and back. And I did other things like rowing boats, guiding, underwater swimming. And when I needed that strength, I had it right down to the last niche. There was no margin between me bein' alive or dead. No margin. I'd just made it on the side of life. And there was something else, too, about that experience.

When I was down that last time and I was ready to give up, you know, I thought, where am I gonna wind up in eternity? Now that was a good question to ask myself. Because basically I was what you'd probably call a self-righteous person. If I wanted to fight, I wouldn't go out and pick one, but I just knew how to get one. You know what I mean. (laughter) I had ego and pride and things like that. Now I did have good morals. I didn't smoke. I didn't drink. I didn't cuss. I didn't tell dirty jokes—I didn't even *listen* to 'em. So basically, I was a pretty decent guy, see. But then, when it came time to die, I wasn't so sure. I said, hey—I didn't say it this way, but I'll say it to you—I said, hey, there's something missing. I don't have any assurance of anything. And I think that has a lot to do with me making it or breaking it too.

Well, I mentioned about the fact that I thought I had it timed to come out behind that paddle wheel. But instead I came right smack up into the center. You know, it took me years to reason out what had happened—all my instincts kept telling me I had everything in the proper order. That current was going so fast downstream that it offset the speed of the steamboat. That steamboat hadn't reached full speed yet; it was still in the process of generating up speed. And at that particular time, the current and the steamboat were traveling at about the same speed. I wasn't taking into consideration the speed of the current. And that's how I missed my judgment. But there were no broken bones. Just surface bruises, and the hide peeled off of all the spots where I'd been hit. I did have a back injury, though, that turned up years later and I had to get chiropractic treatments for it. But no broken bones. I don't think I've ever had a broken bone in my life.

But, anyway, the next day, why, I had lunch with the Captain. They had reached their destination. So then I broke tow with 'em. And I signed a statement saying that he didn't know that I had hitched on, which *he* didn't. That it had all happened in the dark and the shuffle when they made tow. That was to clear him. And he says, in a couple of days this news is gonna be all up and down the river. And you know, I was so embarrassed about this situation that I never even wrote it up in my log. (laughter) I thought I was gonna keep it to myself. I mean, that shows you how silly I was thinking.

IX

Here I am, a landlubber from Minnesota, the lake country, and for me the south country, in that era of time, seemed about as far away as China. I'd heard about different things, malaria fever and so forth, when I was reading up on archaeology in high school. I remembered something about two archaeologists. They were digging in the Yucatan and they both got malaria. But they said that the fever will only hit every third day. After you pass the fever, you'll be good for a couple of days. Then in about three days, it comes back again. And so they had their malaria lined up in such a way that one of 'em would be on his feet and could take care of the other while the other one was down. And I remembered that, but that was all I knew about malaria fever. When it came to malaria fever, why, you'd think in terms of the Yucatan, Central or South America. Some place like that. I wasn't thinking in terms of the southern part of this country. And so I wasn't at all prepared for malaria fever. Not in the least.

I got to feeling real rough. And I was talkin' to a guy, a fisherman, as I was traveling along for a short distance with 'm and visiting as we went. And he diagnosed what I told him about how I felt as malaria fever. He told me how to check it out, and what to expect, and how to determine whether it was or not. And sure enough, it turned out to be malaria fever. So I got some stuff to take for it, quinine capsules, and kept it under control. Until I run out of capsules. Then I got to feeling better, and I more or less passed it off.

Now, uh, I'm about ten miles from New Orleans, maybe a little farther; I'd just passed a ferry crossing called Donaldsonville. And I'm down below that, and there's a lot of upstream wind. I'm below Baton Rouge and now I'm seeing ocean liners on the river and transport ships. And I'm having a rough time making it, so I take the inside of the channel and I'd get out—on days when there was a heavy upstream wind— and I would pull my boat, waist deep, on along the shore on the inside of the banks. That was the shortcut. After I would go so far, I'd cut across to the high spot on the other bend and stretch it out. Just cut across the channel again and again from inside to inside. You're out of the current, but you're cuttin' off a lot of miles. I'd be pulling my boat, and I remember when I'd stop, the shrimp would come up and start nibbling on me. I had to keep moving down. Always something, you know. Then I'd get in and I had a pole and I'd pole it. I tried different things like that. I'd scull it, and one thing and another.

Finally I made it down to a place where they was pumping water for their rice paddies out of the river, a pumping station, and I tied up there. I met a kid and I run around with him a little bit. I was out of quinine and the fever had kicked up on me again and they gave me some raw quinine. Now I always heard that that was bitter. That most people didn't like to take it. I remember how I used to have to take ginger tea when I was a kid. But I mixed this old raw quinine up and I drank it down. And I lay down on my sailboat that night.

The mosquitoes were about ready to eat me alive; they're swarming all over me. You can imagine what kind of mosquito country I was in—that's down in that rice country where they have these rice paddies. And I'm lying in there and I pull this old army blanket up over my head and I'm all hot and sweaty and burnin' up and I pass out. And about dawn the next day I come to. And I feel so relieved and cool, and everything's ever so nice. Then I go to throw my blanket off and it's heavier than lead. I had perspired so much in that blanket that I'd wrapped around me that night that it was absolutely soaked. Just saturated with perspiration. And I had been completely unconscious for all those hours, about twelve hours. Lying in my little sailboat, along the Mississippi River, all by my lonesome with probably nobody knowing anything about it. So finished off that I didn't have strength to go. Well, I untied my sailboat, pushed her out into the river, and took off. And kept working my way down.

I remember when I got inside ten miles above New Orleans, I was out on the river, and it was pitch black night, and I was tryin' to make the last leg. Pushing my way pretty hard. You didn't have snags to worry about, so you could travel on the river at night because it was a deep channel. And you had banks right up to the levees. So, I was out there and a swarm of mosquitoes come down on top of me. And they was so thick that I couldn't even breath without breathin' em in, and I was choking and gagging on 'em. And I hurried up and pulled my handkerchief out and made a mask over my face and tied it. And, uh, there was a barge coming down on me. I wanted to jump in the river to get away from the mosquitoes, but I couldn't because there was this barge coming down. And my flashlight didn't want to go on, and I banged it against my knee a couple of times and stuck it up and waved it at the pilot. The pilot shot his lights down over the end of his barges, and he was practically on top of me. I just barely had a chance to side-step him. And I'd gotten ahold of some kind of mosquito repellentlike stuff. It was kind of Mentholatum-type salve, and my face was all sun-burned, and I took that stuff, and I smeared it all over my face. And it burned like fire, And I smeared it on my feet because, oh, they was running away with my bare feet, you know. And the mosquitoes—it didn't even repel 'em. They just stuck on it like flypaper, and then wiggled around on it. (laughter) But I sidestepped that barge, and he went on down. And that was right after I had been passed out that night along the bank. So, the next day, I think, I made it into New Orleans and docked. And I remember when I come down there past a banana boat, they lowered me a stock of bananas. Hey, I was in dreamland. Man, those were tree-ripened bananas. And some of those bananas on there were as big as my wrist. And, my word, man, I'm telling you, I ate bananas till they stuck out my ears. I thought I was starting to get into paradise! (laughter)

Well, anyway, after I docked in New Orleans at the Canal Street docks—the White Way of the South, they call it—there was things written up about me in the newspapers and all. And I sold my boat to a

fella, and I found out later that he had connections in the underworld. Now that was my first brush with so-called underworld life. But that's another story in itself. That all belongs in another tale that'll have to wait for another time.

RAYMOND KURTZ, SR., never lost his love for adventure. Following the Mississippi solo trip, he bicycled from Chicago throughout the Southwest and later made a canoe trip with his best friend, Julian Fink, all the way from Eden Valley, Minnesota, down the Mississippi to the Gulf of Mexico. He served as an aerial combat photographer with the Navy in the Pacific during World War II. He married Eunice Blackwell in 1943. Their marriage was blessed with three children. He is now owner and operator of Royal Drain Cleaning in Emporia, Kansas.

MARK SCHEEL is a free-lance writer and an information specialist with the Johnson County Library in Shawnee Mission, Kansas. His stories, articles and poems have appeared in numerous magazines including the *Kansas City Star Magazine* and *Kansas Quarterly*. He is also the library liaison for *Potpourri* literary magazine.

PETE PETERSON is a free-lance artist based in Olathe, Kansas. His artwork, often depicting his Native American heritage, has appeared in such national publications as Time-Life Books and is displayed in many collections throughout the nation and abroad.